# A
# f
# ABOVE

D0104368

# Ike Ugochuku

# Tabel of Contents

# CHAPTER 1

## Settling Down in a New School

It was a Saturday and Tony thought about school for the up-coming week. It was a new school and he noticed that kids formed little groups in the class. Just 7 years old, he had received Jesus as his Lord and savior when he was 5 years old. He thought to himself, "I wonder which group I should join?"

There were the ones who felt they were the coolest

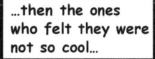

...then the ones who felt they were not so cool...

...and then there were the ones who didn't fit in either.

Tony decided he would join the cool kids crowd. "Yes," he said to himself, "I am for Jesus and I am cool!" He looked forward to school. He would go and play with Femi, Amanda, and Rosalito on Monday.

On Monday, during recess, Tony came out of class to the playground. As he walked to Femi's group, he noticed a boy sitting quietly at a corner of the playground, no one was playing with him. Tony decided to go over and talk with this boy.

"Hello, my name is Tony, what's your name?" "Joshua" he said in a rather dry uninterested voice.

But Tony did not move away. Do you want to play?

Sure!

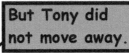

They played together on the playground with some other kids. Tony was glad he had found a new friend and forgot for that day about his plan to join the cool kids.

The next day, during classes, the teacher, Miss Owanda, was teaching about science and Femi was talking with Amanda.

Femi! Stop what you are doing with Amanda!

Femi replied in a rather loud and disrespectful manner, "What you are teaching is so boring."

Miss Owanda did not get upset but in a calm manner she said, "tell me about something you find interesting."

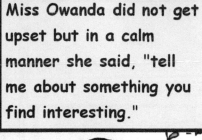

I like to play!

nice!

YEAH!

I like to **party**, have **fun!**

YEAH! right on!

HI-FIVE!

YEAH! —

HA HA! SWEET!

YEAH!

WAP

PAR-TY! PAR-TY!

Class, what do you find interesting?

Tony wanted to say "I like the children's church on Sunday" but he felt that would be out of place and he would look strange so he keeps quiet.

One of the not-so-cool kids, Shade, says, "I like to read" and gets no cheers in the class.

boring

That's very good Shade, playing is good and there is a time for playing but reading can also be fun and it gives you many more options in your future life than just playing.

# CHAPTER 2

## Getting to Know Joshua

At recess time, Tony starts walking out of the class and then sees Joshua. "Hi, Joshua." He is happy to see his friend and they walk out to the playground together.

As they get to the ground, he sees the cool kids playing at the corner and Tony's heart yearns for some sort of attention from them.

I wish I was over there. I wish they would accept me.

But they ignore him. He has a great time playing with Joshua.

They talk about their families a lot.

I have told my Mum and Dad about you, I want to visit you this weekend.

Sure! That would be awesome! I will show you some of my new toys and games. I have this game my Dad just got me, you can shoot monsters. And Mum just bought this new cartoon video on wizards and witches!

The look on Tony's face shows a yucky gaze. Tony's parents do not buy toys or games with monsters for him.

Tony does not like such toys and the monster images do not resonate with his spirit. Tony knows witches and wizards are not of God but he wonders if telling Joshua will end their friendship.

He remembers what his Dad has told him, "Listen to the Holy Spirit dwelling in your heart."

Suddenly, he gets the courage to speak.

I don't watch wizards and witches because it does not portray Christ, but I am sure there are other fun things that we can do together.

Joshua does not know what to say, he does not understand the statement from Tony, after all everyone he knows is excited about wizards and witches but he likes Tony, he does not feel condemnation from him, but he is different.

Yes, we will definitely find things to do!

Tony's Mum comes to pick him up and sees him standing with Joshua.

Hello, Tony

Hi, Mum

How was your day in School?

Good

Joshua and I played, I want to see him this weekend, is that okay?

Well, I would need to speak with his parents and find out some more about them. Your Dad and I need to know some more about the people you will be visiting. Remember, you will be visiting a family not just Joshua.

When they get home, Tony's Mum and Dad discuss and agree that Tony's Mum should call Joshua's house.

Tony's Mum calls. The phone is answered by Joshua's Mum, Mrs Uwadi.

Hello?

Hello, my name is Mrs Friedman, can I Speak with Mrs Uwadi?

Hi, Mrs Friedman, my son has told me a lot about your son Tony. How are you?

I am well.

Oh, please call me Yinka, so I hope everything is okay?

Everything is okay, Yinka, please call me Sarah. I am calling because the kids discussed and Tony would like to visit Joshua.

# CHAPTER 3

## Getting Noticed by the Cool Kids

The next day, Joshua and Tony meet each other and bounce happily together into school.

During class, Miss Owanda is teaching mathematics.

circle

What is a circumference?

The length of a circle, Miss Owanda!

Can anyone solve this problem on the board?

15x + 7 = 22
what is x?

No one answers, then Tony gets up and solves the problem.

5x + 7 = 22
what is x?

That is very good work, Tony!

As Tony walks back to his desk he gets a high five from Rosalito.

wrap nice!

It makes him feel good.

The recess bell rings and as kids in the class gather their items to go out to play, Rosalito comes over to Tony and says "why don't you join us and play today?"

Tony forgets about Joshua and happily joins the cool kids to play during the break.

Joshua notices that Tony is not playing with him, but he says "Tony has other friends."

While Tony was playing with the cool kids, Femi said to Rosalito, "Look at Drew over there, he doesn't know how to climb, what a weak boy!"

They all laughed and Tony found himself laughing reluctantly.

He felt bad inside. "How can I be laughing at Drew; he has done nothing wrong. I should go and help him."

But there was the conflict with the desire to belong to the group. "If I go over there, I would be different and the cool kids will not accept me."

So he did nothing except join the cool kids as they played and sometimes made horrible remarks about other people.

At the end of the day, Tony had conflicts within.

As he came into his Mum's car, he looked a bit sad.

# CHAPTER 4

## A Visit to Joshua's House

On Saturday, Sarah and Tony arrive at Joshua's place. Yinka answers the door and Joshua is just behind her. Tony and Joshua go upstairs to play.

Come and have something to drink.

Thanks, I will have some tea.

So how do you like this area?

Its nice, the people are friendly.

Meanwhile, Tony and Joshua try to find a game. "I have a battleship set," says Joshua, "lets play that." So they play for about an hour,

then they come downstairs. Sarah has left.

It was nice talking with your Mum, Tony. Why don't you guys go out to the yard and play?

Joshua has a soccer ball, they play soccer.

Then they come indoors and have lunch.

Then they watch some cartoons. Joshua lets Tony choose since he told him he filters what he watches.

It was a great time for the two friends and Sarah comes back in the evening to pick Tony up.

I would like to visit Tony next Saturday.

That sounds very good, Joshua. Tell your Mum to call me and we will make arrangements.

How did you find it?

It was good Mum, I had a lot of fun!

# CHAPTER 5

## Invitation to the Cool Kids Party

The next Monday in school, Amanda comes over to Tony and says, "its my birthday party next Saturday, you are invited".

Tony is excited, "Yes!" he says to himself, "I am accepted!"

Sure, I will come Amanda, but I have to ask my Mum.

"Whatever." Amanda replies. Asking parents for permission to attend a party was not her style.

Tony gets the message and somehow feels a conflict going on within himself but he walks away leaving the topic unresolved.

Hi Joshua, so I will see you on Saturday. Your Mum says she will drop you off.

Yes, I am looking forward to that!

Amanda invited me to her birthday party, can I go?

Well, do we know Amanda?

No, but she is in my class and I would really like to go, lots of people in class will be there.

Will Joshua be there?

I don't think Joshua was invited but I would still like to go.

Sarah senses a conflict in her heart, on one hand she would like Tony to feel accepted and not left out, on the other hand, she does not know Amanda or the kids who will be at that party. "Okay, I will discuss with your Dad" says Sarah.

When Tony's Dad returns home, Sarah discusses with him and they agree that Sarah should chaperon Tony.

So they call Tony. Dad says "Tony, you know we like to know a family before you go over to them, well because this is a gathering we will allow you to go this time, but your Mum will be there with you". Tony wondered how he would look at the party but at least he would be there, so he said "Thank you, Mum and Dad".

# CHAPTER 6

## Joshua Visits Tony's House

On Saturday, Joshua comes to Tony's house. Yinka drops him at the door.

Lets watch some DVDs!

They watch some Christian animated series such as "Paws and Tales" and torchlighters (John Wesley). Joshua enjoys the DVDs so much.

After watching the DVDs, he asks about John Wesley. "He cared so much about God? Why?"

Tony is excited to talk about Jesus.

Well, God created us and made our hearts like a house for him to live in. So we always have that empty feeling in our hearts, like an empty house, until we invite him to come and live in our hearts. John Wesley thought religion would fill that gap but it did not, it wasn't till he asked Jesus into his heart that he found peace and could have a real friendship with God.

Joshua looked at him, thinking, "how can that be possible?"

Have you ever asked Jesus to come into your heart and live?

No...

...we never talk about it in my house. We do go Church but I can see you and John Wesley have something different.

I asked him to come and live in my heart when I was five years old. It's such a wonderful peace one has.

Do you want to have some snacks?

Of course!

They run along and have some cookies and juice.

After that, they go out to the yard and play in the trees.

# CHAPTER 7

## Conflict at Amanda's Party

The next Saturday, Tony dresses up for the party.

He says a prayer before going:

Lord, give me favor in the eyes of the people there and give me the boldness to proclaim your name.

He arrives there with Sarah. They have food, drinks and games. It's a lot of fun, but somehow Tony feels out of place, like he is not supposed to be there.

During the party there is a game called "Follow the Witch." Amanda, the birthday girl, dresses up as a witch and the rest of the people in the party are supposed to follow her and sing along.

Tony feels very uncomfortable with this game. He thinks to himself "I am a follower of Christ...

...not a follower of Witches."

He turns and looks at his Mum Sarah and she beckons to him to come to her.

So he stays with her while this game is being played. He is the only kid that does not take part. Sarah hugs him to give him assurance that she accepts him.

During the party, Tony feels a struggle within himself. Sarah asks him as they get into the car to leave the party, "Did you have fun today?" "Yes, Mum" Tony replies in a dry manner.

Remember God loves you more than anyone in this world, more than even I love you and you know I love you a lot.

Keep your eyes always on him, he has everything you need or want.

Thank you, Mum

When Tony gets home, he talks with his Dad.

Daddy, do you ever have conflicts at your workplace with who you are in Christ?

# CHAPTER 8

## Spiritual Connection with Joshua

The next school day, during recess, Tony rushes to Joshua and they go by the corner to talk.

How was the birthday party?

It was okay.

It doesn't seem like you enjoyed it so much.

Well, I just feel that it conflicts with who I am in Christ.

What do you mean?

Well, Christ takes us out of the world when we invite him into our heart and brings us into the kingdom of God, so it seems I can't really enjoy things of the world.

Tony, I have been thinking about what you told me in your house, that God can live in your heart, why and how?

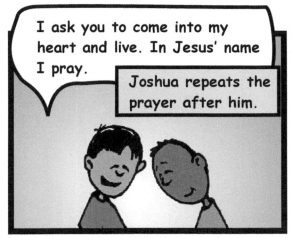

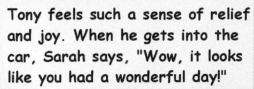

Immediately, Sarah says a prayer while driving. "Father, thank you for the new person in the family of God. We pray that Joshua would enjoy fellowship with you and be a light in his home in Jesus' name."

# CHAPTER 9

## Accepted from Above

The next day in school, Tony sees Joshua as they walk into the classroom.

Hi, Joshua, my brother and friend!

During recess, Femi comes over to Tony.

Hey Tony, are you coming to play with us?

No, thanks. I will be playing with my brother and friend, Joshua!

Brother?! I didn't know you have the same parents!

Yes, we do! We are of the family of Christ!

Femi says "Oh" and gives a strange look...

...but Tony doesn't pay any attention and walks to the playground with Joshua. He has no pull in his heart to belong to the cool kids and he is happy with peace in his heart.